HOW TO CHANGE
THE WORLD
WHILE WAITING FOR YOUR TOAST

HOW TO CHANGE
THE WORLD
WHILE WAITING FOR YOUR TOAST

By Randy Friesen and Mark Wardell

© Copyright 2004 mr.e Publishing

No part of this publication may be reproduced, stored in a retrieval system, or transmitted, in any form or by any other means, electronic, mechanical, photocopying, recording, or otherwise, without the written prior permission of the author.

Printed in Victoria, Canada

Book design by Goodhorse Design (www.goodhorse.ca)
Cover design by Circle Graphics (www.circlegraphics.ca)

Note for Librarians: a cataloguing record for this book that includes Dewey Classification and US Library of Congress numbers is available from the National Library of Canada. The complete cataloguing record can be obtained from the National Library's online database at:
www.nlc-bnc.ca/amicus/index-e.html

ISBN 1-4120-3538-4

Printed in Abbotsford, BC, Canada

Dedication

Writing a book while building a business is not an easy task. With young families in addition, the task would have been insurmountable without the support and encouragement of our wives and children.

To our wives especially, we want to thank you publicly for everything you do behind the scenes to continue to propel us to success and excellence.

- Randy and Mark

Table of Contents

Introduction 1

Cheaper by the Dozen 5

Hit it Hard and Coast! 15

Viewer or Doer 31

Volume is Good, but Hair is Bad 37

Bring it Home 45

70 Things to do Now That I'm 70 51

It's All About Trust 59

Do the POLC-A 67

10 Minutes to Learn the Tkatchev 79

The Freedom of Structure 85

Decision Making – Toast Style! 91

Breaking Down the Barriers 99

Taking Action 113

Introduction

This book is purposely short. It is meant for people who don't have time to read. If that's you....this book is written for you. Take an hour, grab a coffee and read. While you are reading, have a pen handy. You'll come up with some ideas that will change your world. Write them down in the book. It's easy, quick and it could change your entire situation or business as you know it.

People have asked us if this is a business book or a personal growth book. Our answer is simple. It's both! As business consultants we do something unique when starting a working relationship with a company. We begin with the business owner. What is their personal mission in life? What are their personal goals? We believe that who we are as people drives who we are in the workplace or who we are as business owners.

This book specifically focuses on capturing moments of time and then applying that captured time to something of lasting value. In many cases the time needed to spawn a thought that will change the world is just about the time you wait for your toast to pop out of the toaster! We hope you enjoy the read.

Randy's side of the story...

This book outline began on a two day getaway with my wife for her birthday. Since then the outline changed a number of times as thoughts and stories were exchanged with my friend and business colleague Mark Wardell. What has finally evolved is a book that we are both proud of. It's full of practical suggestions you can use to change your business and change your life. But back to my wife! While on this little getaway in the big city, she was doing some clothes shopping. This led to me having some time on my hands sitting in the proverbial 'husband' chair outside various changing rooms. I used the time to corral my thoughts writing them down on a pad of paper that I quickly hid inside my shirt pocket whenever the model came out of her fitting room. As soon as she disappeared the pen and pad came out again. My first working title was "How to change your life while waiting for your wife to try on clothes". After some careful consideration, a couple of cuffs on the head from my wife and a realization that we would be alienating half of the world with that title, my partner Mark, pulled me away from the abyss! Little did I know, I would be waiting yet again a few days later. This time it was for some toast and I again used the time to change my world. This book will show you how to use the most innocuous time to change your business or change your world. You will discover time you never thought you had. It may be just a piece of toast away!

Mark's side of the story...

Coaching was my chosen profession through University and became my full time passion when I completed. Taking young gymnasts to the national level of competition was an accomplishment that has stayed with me throughout my life. In the world of athletics, the management of resources is crucial. How much time to practise; what to practise; how to practice. Some very basic questions, but the answers to which changed everything in the success of my athletes and my success and fulfillment as a coach. Everything I learned through coaching in the athletic arena I have brought with

4 me into the business world and more. As a company, we are dedicated to learning new things all the time. At the very core of the business experience and human experience is the management of time. How do we use our time every day? Are we investing it or simply spending it? Can the simple two minutes spent waiting for your toast really change your business and change your life?

We certainly think so!

Chapter 1

Cheaper by the Dozen

"I'm doing your favourite thing Dad," 12-year-old Max explained eagerly.

"Really? What's that?" I replied, trying to figure out exactly what piece of information I had harpooned his way had hit the target.

"I'm multitasking," Max said confidently.

"Multitasking? What exactly are you doing?"

"Just like you said Dad, I'm doing two things at once. I've got the oatmeal cooking in the microwave and at the same time I'm doing the toast in the toaster oven. The cool thing is that I'm doing two things at once, but I'm only working as hard as I would if I was doing one thing."

That was a defining moment for this young man. The understanding that to succeed you had to learn to multiply your efforts. Not just work harder, but be smarter at your work.

A successful financial analyst was drowning in his own business. Working incredibly long hours and putting in excessive amounts of sweat and tears, he found it still wasn't enough. Despite his efforts, his growth rate was slowing and his family time was disintegrating. If he kept up this pace for much longer, either he or his business was going to break...quite possibly both.

This story has a happy ending however. By using straightforward techniques like delegating and designing systems, he was finally able to concentrate on the important aspects of his business, changing his world dramatically.

The point is that the changes weren't exactly rocket science or difficult to implement. They just needed to be applied consistently over time. But you don't have any time right? That's a huge problem facing many business managers and owners. They are out of time. They are washing dishes and fixing engines when they should be building their business. They are like the passengers on the Titanic. Many people went about their day, refusing to admit that anything was wrong as massive ship (read business!) plummeted into the icy Atlantic.

Is your business drowning?

Are you working hard at home or at the office without feeling successful?

Are you looking for some practical solutions without a lot of 'consultant speak'?

Are you ready to take charge of your life?

Then read on!

This book is dedicated to those who want to change their lives, change their businesses and change their world.

It starts with as much time as it takes to wait for your toast!

What is the value of time? We've all heard that time is precious but what does that really mean? Much of the understanding of time comes from our perspective of time. What does that mean? If you ever have had a brush with death, or had an experience with somebody leaving this earth unexpectedly, you know what perspective means. It makes you look at life in a different way. It changes the perception of how you see events or relationships.

There does come a time when life is over, but as a society we tend to believe that we will live forever, or at least it is easy to get caught up in that thinking. Wasting time can easily become a habit that is ingrained to the point where we reach retirement or worse yet, the end of our lives and wonder what we've done. Have you ever had a day where you've sat in your office at 5 p.m. and couldn't figure out what you actually had accomplished? You've been exceptionally busy, but what had you really gained towards your ultimate goals?

Peter Legge, a brilliant international speaker and successful businessman provided some perspective in one of his keynote addresses. He suggested that the average human today is around for 80 years. Sounds like a lot. A fair bit of time to waste and you'll still have plenty of years left. What he said next however, brought the perspective home.

Eighty years is only 4,160 weeks. Wow!

Now calculate your age and think about how many weeks you have left on this planet! We are betting you want to make them count.

This chapter is dedicated to the value of time. One of the greatest books ever written about the value of time from a business and human perspective was *Cheaper by the Dozen*. This book, written by the children of Frank and Lillith Gilbreth, is a biography of two of the early pioneers of motion study.

This couple made ground breaking inroads into the study of how processes and business could operate more efficiently and more profitably. Frank Gilbreth was the first to conduct experiments with putting a string of light bulbs on employees and filming them. Analyzing the film would then give him great insights into how motions and repetitive action could be done more efficiently and effectively. He carried these principles into his home life where he and his wife had 12 children. One of the stories had Mr. Gilbreth shaving with two razors to improve his speed. He did improve his speed but inevitably returned to just one razor as he spent too much time repairing himself after the occasional cut!

His exceptionally scientific approach was combined with Mrs. Gilbreth's more human approach as she was a well educated psychologist. The success they shared as a couple with their family and their success in business should not be overlooked. It is definitely a book worth reading. The marriage of a scientific approach with a human and people relationship approach is exceptionally powerful.

One of the biggest barriers to the success of a business venture is the inability of a business owner to let go. They keep a watchful eye on everything, afraid that if they don't, things will begin to unravel. Of course with this approach, a business owner can still grow a business to a certain level, but inevitably it will reach a very critical stage.

We call it the glass ceiling. You can see the future, you know where you want to go, but why can't you get there? Why can't you break through the barrier?

> Chris was a mechanic. He loved working on cars. That was his passion and he was good at it. As more people heard about his work, more people brought their cars to him. That's great news right? Sure, but Chris couldn't keep up with the new business. So like any good business owner would, he hired some other mechanics. He trained them but was very meticulous about the quality of his product. So, he oversaw every aspect of the work to the point where he wasn't doing any mechanical work himself and the new mechanics became very frustrated at having Chris breathing down their necks every day. In the end, the business imploded. The business came crashing in on itself because Chris could not let go. He couldn't make the transition from the person "doing" the job, to the person "managing" the job.

Alex worked in a computer firm. She was an excellent programmer. Her bosses saw her work and were impressed. Alex was promoted to manager of her group. This was something that Alex had always thought would make her happy. She was climbing the corporate ladder! However, her work now consisted of managing other people's efforts. She hated it! She wanted to go back to programming and she did. For her that was the right decision.

Alex and Chris both hit the glass ceiling. They reached a place where they could not climb any further without changing. In both of these situations, the end result was to go back to a place where they were comfortable. This is not a bad thing! It just needs to be recognized. More business owners need to understand what they want out of their business. Once this is understood, the plan for action can be drawn out.

If that plan calls for business expansion, then a completely new perspective must be developed. Instead of being the one 'doing' all the work directly, the business owner must be the one 'managing' all the work.

This is an exceptionally key difference. It also calls for a completely new perspective on how to manage time.

In many businesses that fail, the owners worked very hard. They worked exceptionally long hours doing everything from sweeping floors to dealing with customers to bookkeeping.

But how much time did they spend growing their business?

Were they able to see the difference between working in the business and managing the business?

In many cases the answer is sadly, "No."

Most business owners simply complete a task. The owner of a hair salon is a stylist. The owner of an architect firm is an architect. Of course, you say, that is the way it has to be.

Yes, the owner of an architect firm will usually be an architect, but if he or she wants to propel the business beyond a one-person shop, they need to see themselves as a business owner and manager. This is absolutely key.

Once this new perspective is gained, the ability to implement time saving systems and techniques is a natural fit.

One times one will always equal one. The business owner must think beyond themselves to the world of multi-tasking and multiplication.

How can I make the small time count?

How can I get a lot of little things to add up to one big business success?

The discovery of the answers to these questions is the key to growing the business into the success you have always dreamed of!

HOW TO CHANGE THE WORLD WHILE WAITING FOR YOUR TOAST

Hit it Hard and Coast!

One of the greatest gifts you can give your employees is the example of working and working hard.

As a company we encourage our staff to read books and magazines. We especially encourage the reading of biographies. The insight you gain into why people became successful is amazing. One trait that comes back again and again is the concept of work.

You must work hard! Is this a contradiction to applying 'smart' working techniques and the ability to 'multi-task'? Absolutely not. We believe there is a fundamental issue with those who succeed and those who don't. How hard are you going to work? Multi-tasking multiplies your efforts, which is ideal, but you need the engine of work behind the multi-tasking.

16 Randy's story

In my teens I worked in a large family-owned supermarket. I worked my way onto the night shift. An older gentleman by the name of Ralph worked with us. Ralph was one of those guys that you knew could give you some nuggets about life that would help set your life direction. He didn't work at the store because he had to. He already owned several apartment buildings and was quite wealthy. He told us he worked at the store because of the insurance benefits for his family. I believe one of his real reasons for being there was to be a mentor and coach to the younger store employees. He was a natural at it, and I think it gave him a lot of fulfilment to operate in that role.

One of the greatest things he ever said to me has stuck to this day and has multiplied itself 100 times over in the classroom and with business clients.

Each week the grocery store would receive its shipments of goods from the wholesaler. The big semi truck would back up to the loading dock and 10-20 skids full of groceries in various shapes and sizes would be taken by forklift from the truck into the store warehouse. It was the job of the night shift to get the product on the store floor and fill up the shelves. Every single load night, week after week, Ralph would use the same phrase. He would say, "Tonight boys, let's hit it hard and coast."

What does this mean? Well for us in the grocery store the meaning was pretty straight forward. Let's get this load out on the store floor, fill up the shelves and then we can relax a little bit. But it was more than just being quick and then slacking off. Ralph lived the slogan. He would work very hard and do excellent work. The emphasis was on the work first…then on the reward. The faster and more efficient we were led to more time at a relaxed pace later. As simple as that philosophy was, it worked. Western society today can be heavily focused on the reward first and then the work. Buying goods on credit, no payments for six months, money advances on paychecks. These are all examples of rewarding first and paying later. The philosophy permeates our culture. The "hit it hard and coast" philosophy emphasizes work…hard work. That is an important key. When I took over the management of the night shift, guess which phrase I used every single load night, week after week? "Hit it hard and coast!"

Now how can you hit it hard in your business? One of the ways is to grab opportunities immediately and don't let a minute slip away.

We researched a successful owner of a wedding planning and catering business. Her rule of thumb was very simple. Do everything you could now. If it could be done now, don't wait. That meant if it was only 9 a.m. but there was an opportunity to have the dinner plates set out and arranged, she'd do it. She was constantly looking for opportunities to get things done immediately. Whatever could be done in advance would be done in advance.

In her business she knew that problems would occur. She couldn't prepare for the exact problem, but she could prepare to be ready to deal with problems. Notice the subtle difference there? Think about your business. Are problems going to arise? Inevitably they are. It may be difficult to project what these problems will be, but you can plan to be prepared to deal with them.

A number of our clients tell us at the beginning of our working relationship that they deal with issues as they come up. It is not uncommon for people to run their businesses and their personal lives exactly in this manner. Their 'plan' is just to take things day by day and hope for the best. Financial planners tell us the majority of people in the Western world have no plan for their retirement years in terms of finances. Think about it. What is the one inevitable thing that is going to happen to all of us whether we want it to happen or not? We will all become older and then we will all die. It will happen! If we're not planning for something that obvious, why would we plan for anything else? And that seems to be exactly how many people live.

Our message here is to **live on purpose**! Do things on purpose…don't let things just happen. Take an active role in your personal future and take an active role in the future of your business.

One of the things that we do again and again with clients is review their personal goals. We put it together in what we call a Life Map.

We ask business owners to discuss their goals:

What are your personal goals?

Personal goals are your self-improvement goals. Examples include: educational goals such as degrees or diplomas; skill goals such as learning to play an instrument or learning to speed read; personal development goals such as controlling your anger, fitness goals and so forth.

What are your people goals?

People goals are your relationship goals. Examples include family goals, friendship goals, romantic goals, people you'd like to meet, people you'd like to work with, people you'd like to learn from, and so forth.

What are your play goals?

Play goals are your enjoyment goals, your fun goals. Life would be dull without them. They include places you'd like to visit, activities you'd like to engage in, things you'd like to purchase and so on. Would you like a cabin on a lake or brand new Mercedes? Would you like to go sailing in the Caribbean or hiking in the Himalayas? It's your life and you have a right to enjoy it!

What are your professional goals?

Professional goals are your work and financial goals. Examples include personal income goals, investment goals, business goals, financial independence goals, amount of time devoted to work, type of work done and so forth.

What are your public goals?

Public goals are your contribution goals. They are the things you would like to give back to society. You may wish to volunteer your time at your local food bank, you may wish to make a financial contribution to cancer research, or you may wish to take a group of Scouts camping. You're going to feel great about this list.

Take a moment right now to think about your goals. What do you want to do this year? What about next? This is not new advice. Business and personal growth experts have been telling people for years to write their goals down. It is extremely powerful. What makes things even more powerful is to ensure your goals are measurable and definable. 'Being a great mother' or 'Having a great business' are lofty thoughts, but are they really goals? We would argue that they have to be much more defined. How are you going to be a great mother? What does that really mean in the first place? For example, if that means spending more time with the kids, how much more time? Does it mean group time or individual time? Does it mean a family vacation or movie night? How often should this happen?

Once these questions are answered, you can come up with a much more defined and therefore measurable goal. An example could be:

> "My goal is to spend one hour per week one-on-one with each of my children doing a specific activity like reading, going out for dessert, or playing a board game."

Now that's definable! You can measure that. And the goal is broken down to a point where it becomes very realistic in carrying out.

The business aspect is quite similar. What does 'having a great business' really mean? Does it mean the owner wants to work 40 hours a week or less? Does it mean that the business needs to make over $10 million in annual sales? Does it mean that there is a business that can be handed down to children in 15 years?

What we've found through our experience is that many goals are never actioned because they were never defined properly in the first place.

A lot of people have great dreams of success. But what does that really mean? It's only once they've been defined and broken down that you can really have a shot at fulfilling your personal and entrepreneurial goals.

Take a moment right now to think about your personal goals. Better yet, get a pen and write them down in the space provided.

Use this book as a guide and review your goals over the next couple of years. You'll be absolutely amazed at what you'll be able to accomplish.

Personal Goals

_____
_____
_____
_____
_____
_____

People Goals

_____
_____
_____
_____
_____
_____
_____

Play Goals

_____
_____
_____
_____
_____
_____

Professional Goals

_____
_____
_____
_____
_____
_____

Public Goals

_____
_____
_____
_____
_____
_____

Hit it Hard and Coast!

How are you preparing for the future? What can you do now that will help shape the future for yourself or your business? Have you ever had those moments where you thought of something important you had to do, and then talked yourself out of it for a moment to handle another urgent issue, only to never complete your original task?

A television news piece recently profiled a family returning to their home after a devastating forest fire. A group of homes had been totally destroyed. Only the scarred chimney bricks were left. You couldn't help but have your heart sink as the woman who owned the property explained that she didn't have insurance. She had a number of very sad excuses (including a death in the family) about why she had neglected to renew her insurance, but none of those excuses, regardless of how tragic they were, could bring back the fact that the insurance hadn't been renewed and her home was a complete loss.

The important rule to remember here is to make the small time count. Yes, it's the time it would take to make a piece of toast! What can you do now? Right now?

Think of something that you've been putting off related to your business life or personal life. An old friend to call or email? A call to check on your business insurance? Stop reading and take action on one item. Just one! Here's the amazing thing. That one item, as small as it seems, can become two items, then three. Soon you will become used to getting things done.

Business mogul Jimmy Pattison heads an empire of 50 companies worldwide, with assets in the billions. His business interests include grocery stores, car dealerships, advertising companies, etc. How does a man who is very involved with his businesses keep up? Firstly, he works exceptionally hard. An article (*Vancouver Province* newspaper, 2000) profiled Jimmy as he jetted around the globe keeping track of his assets and managing his business. He used a system of organization that helped him separate his various business ventures. In the article he was working on five projects, so he had five briefcases on the go. Each one contained pertinent information on that specific project. When he needs to change focus, this effective organizational technique allowed him to do so.

The point that needs to be stressed here is how the physical ties into the mental.

If all the papers from the various projects that you are working on are together in one physical place or space, the chance of something going missing, you wasting invaluable time searching for information or simply being confused as you switch from project to project, is greatly decreased.

Think about the projects you have on the go. Here's a sample list:

- Coaching kid's soccer team
- Business expansion project
- Business accounting project
- Wine making class with spouse

Your list is probably larger and that's ok. The same principles apply. First, physically organize yourself for each project. For example, create a coaching bag for soccer. Your schedule, references, supplies should all be located in one place. Make room for these supplies and ensure that once the practice or a game is over that the gear is stored in the same place every time.

Sound simplistic? Did you know that the average business executive wastes 30 minutes each day looking for lost information? Thirty minutes each day! Do the math. That's like losing one day each month!

If you can cut down on the time spent searching for soccer balls and your coaching clipboard each week, you will gain valuable time.

Do the same with your business ventures. You can be as practical as billionaire Jimmy Pattison. Have a different briefcase or container for different projects. When you need to switch projects, your mind will follow your physical lead of switching containers. It will also save you time and effort in locating everything necessary to work on a project.

After you have organized yourself, one of the most powerful ways to propel your mind forward and begin a task is to start small and start with something physical.

You'll read again and again throughout this book a common theme. These are practical tips for utilizing small amounts of time. We've all heard the term, 'work smarter, not harder.' The term sounds great, and is great, but how do you actually do it? Here is one very practical example.

When you have a task that you need to begin, start by cleaning your desk. If that doesn't sound like much, think about it like this. Success propels your mind forward. Newton's law of motion comes into play here as well. An object in motion tends to stay in motion. An object at rest tends to stay at rest. If

Hit it Hard and Coast!

you can make your mind believe that you have accomplished something; that you have had a victory; that you are winning; you are much more apt to have a success when you tackle your bigger project. Cleaning your desk is easy. Organize your files, throw garbage away, put the pens in the drawer, etc. But once you've built that momentum, it can be transferred to more difficult tasks like writing your company mission statement or preparing for a speech you have to make.

Now, what are you going to do with the time you save? That's the continual question. Sounds like just enough time to make a piece of toast!

HOW TO CHANGE THE WORLD WHILE WAITING FOR YOUR TOAST

Chapter 3

Viewer or Doer

You can love TV! What? In a book that stresses time management principles you can't have a statement like that. TV is the biggest time waster around, isn't it?

First let's explain the chapter title.

You're either a viewer or a doer.

A viewer is someone who:

- Watches life go by.
- Makes excuses.
- Blames the government for all the problems in the world.
- Always has 'issues.'

- Talks down to people.
- Doesn't ask questions.
- Doesn't read books.
- Isn't involved.

A viewer simply watches and criticizes and watches and criticizes and watches some more until it's time to go to bed. They go through life watching and criticizing and basically get to where they get to more by happenstance than perseverance.

A doer on the other hand is a quite a different animal.

A doer:

- Watches and learns.
- Listens and acts.
- Maps out a plan.
- Finds a mentor.
- Asks questions.
- Manages time.
- Constantly looks for ways to change his or her world.

Viewer or Doer

A doer looks to change the world while waiting for the toast!

Fundamentally, people will be either viewers or doers. Think about the people you know and come in contact with.

Do you know people who talk more about excuses rather than accomplishments? Chances are you've found yourself a viewer.

Now is the time, however, to turn the microscope on yourself. We will venture to bet that if you've invested the time to read this far, you are a doer. That's great. But the thing to remember is that we all have viewer and doer attributes.

By nature you are a doer but what do you do that has more viewer characteristics?

Think about the past week.

Think about today.

Were there any periods of time that could have been dealt with differently? Look for patterns. Diving into the TV for a couple of hours after a long work day may feel relaxing, but is it the best use of time? Remember, TV isn't bad, it's all about time. It's much better to have a plan of what to watch at the beginning of the week and then simply follow that plan. You can also turn TV into something more than what it is. Turn it into an event like a family night or even a business opportunity. Watching the 'Waltons' of yesteryear is like today's families watching 'Survivor.' It can be a very positive thing to enjoy a show together as a group with a bowl of popcorn. This ties right into the overriding principle of multi-tasking. Yes, you are watching a TV show, but the family is together as well. Family dinners almost seem to be a thing of the past. Everyone is so busy and has so little time. What ways can you think of to combine an activity **and** include some time with your family or friends?

Taking some business associates or business partners to a sporting event or social event in the same way has now propelled you beyond simply watching.

You are multi-tasking! Think about it. Think about what you could do if you had twice the time you have now. If you can find a way to do two things at once you are doing just that. With a little planning and some perseverance, it's easier than you might think!

Viewer or Doer. Which one do you subscribe to be?

If you really want to boost up your 'doer' attributes here are three practical steps to take your doer status to the next level.

Plan

You've probably heard the expression, "People don't plan to fail, they fail to plan." This time honoured saying is exceptionally valid in today's world. There are so many 'valid' distractions that can take you away from your goal, you must have a plan.

What do you want personally in the next year? Make a list. If you really want to learn to play the guitar in a year, what do you need to do now to make that happen? Have you found an instructor? Have you planned for practise time each day? Have you committed to reaching your goal? It all starts with a plan.

Proceed

Once the plan is in place, you must proceed. You must actually do something. So much time is wasted in corporations big and small by a lot of talking and little doing. It's the doing that will push your business forward. Here's the caution. Doing things on their own merits without a plan is the fast track to disaster. Remember that 80% of businesses fail. In most of those operations there were very hardworking people. But hard work on its own simply doesn't cut it. You must proceed, but only when you have a plan and the work you do is done specifically to fulfill that plan.

Prevail

We must prevail! There are times when we look at business tasks facing us and say, "I don't know how we can pull this one off!" Take this book for example. We knew we needed to write a book as part of the overall Wardell package. But how could this be accomplished? We were growing a business and already working exceptionally hard. This was an opportunity to practise what we preach! First we started with a plan. Chapter titles and chapter outlines were fleshed out. Following that step the work needed to be accomplished. Sitting down to write a book is an enormous undertaking, but sitting down to write a chapter or a few paragraphs is not nearly as difficult. So with an overall plan in place and timelines set, we proceeded. Prevailing comes from continuing to proceed when you think you cannot proceed anymore. This is where athletic training can really come into play. Prevailing is digging down and finding that source of energy when you are at the edge of your limit. How do people climb Mt. Everest? Good planning and then one step at a time.

Chapter 4

Volume is Good, but Hair is Bad

Mothers have often provided some great examples of hard work. This story was shared with us by a business colleague.

His mom was really the first person that taught him about multi-tasking. On a typical weekday morning, she would be making cinnamon buns for breakfast, preparing the roast for dinner, fixing his sister's hair and tidying up the kitchen all at the same time or so it appeared. What that woman could accomplish in a day was incredible. Raising a family on a shoe-string budget was a profound accomplishment.

There was a drawback however.

Occasionally, a hair would somehow end up in the food. With all the buzzing around the kitchen, this could be assumed as an inevitable cost of doing business. It could also be assumed that the level of activity was so high that quality had taken a dip!

How much are you going to sacrifice quality for quantity?

We've worked with companies in similar industries. One does half the sales of the other. Which one is more profitable? Should be the bigger one, right? They have millions more in sales. They have a big office. They do more jobs. Wrong. It's actually the smaller company making the bigger net profits. Remember, at the end of the day it's what you keep that is the most important…not your gross sales!

Pushing only for quantity is usually the fast train to disaster. But let's be very clear about something. When that kind of statement is written, the 'viewer' in us can say, "Maybe I won't work quite so hard today because quantity is not really where it's at." That kind of thinking is a big mistake.

The entire "quality vs. quantity" debate is really not one that can be isolated to rules and strict rights and wrongs. It is really a question of principle and balance. Firstly, how committed am I to the principle of quality in my personal life and my business life? If I'm committed, what level of quantity do I need to produce to ensure that I can build a business but still stay committed to the standard of quality that I've set?

Mark's story

In preparing for a strategic interview that shaped my entrance into the world of business coaching, I needed a suit.

Money at the time was tight. This was a classic case of quantity over quality. I could get six lower priced suits or two ultimate, high-end business suits. I went to the suit shop and tried on the lower-end models. They looked good. They might not last as long. Maybe they didn't have some of the pizzazz of a high-end suit. Maybe they weren't made of Italian fabric, but that's ok, right? No one could really tell. With a nice tie and a nice shirt I was good to go.

Hold it!

My principle on business was to accept only the best. How could I tell a business owner to portray the best but not do so myself? In the end, the high-end business suits were purchased. They cost much more.

But you know what I found out after the key interview I was preparing for? One of the things this business maverick had said to his associate afterwards was, "That guy was wearing a very expensive suit. This was obviously important to him."

That contact inevitably led to my entrance into the business consulting world and began the success we now enjoy as a company. I'll never regret that I chose to go with quality.

Being cheap has a price tag attached to it. It is not a bad thing to pay less for something that is of value, you just need to be very clear on why you are doing what you're doing and make sure you've calculated all the costs.

Let's say you are taking a vacation with your family. You can get a large townhouse just outside of the resort town for $150 a night. You can also stay in a smaller room right in the resort for $200 a night.

The $150 per night place might sound immediately like the better choice. Just make sure you calculate all the costs. Is there a parking charge every time you drive into town? Did you have to bring more of your own supplies to stay in the less expensive place? What about those costs that are not as simple to put a price tag on? What are the external amenities like at both locations? Which one is a better fit? How much will you spend on food at each location?

Volume is Good, but Hair is Bad

The less expensive location may indeed be a better fit, but just make sure you are calculating all the costs and comparing apples to apples.

This approach works very similarly in the business world. Generally, you must pay for quality. Attending a seminar might be a less expensive way for you to get ideas for your business and propel you ahead. Hiring an experienced accountant or having your own personal business consultant may be more expensive. But when you begin to add up the true costs, the second option makes much more sense for many companies.

Why do you think mentorship and coaching are exploding as positive ways to get ahead in today's marketplace?

The obvious answer is that they work.

But we must go beyond. Why do they work? They work because one-on-one relationships build a commitment and level of expectation that forces the business owner or manager to go beyond what they would have done if they did not have the business coach to be accountable to.

In a priceless conversation with a Wardell client, the client, who was in the early stages of the program, asked out loud why he was paying Wardell to do this work. I could do this work myself and save a bunch of money he suggested. The answer was simple. He simply would not do the work if Wardell was not involved. Other things would get in the way.

When asked why he had completed the portion of business development we had just been working on his answer was straightforward. It was because he had a meeting coming up with his Wardell consultant and he wanted to ensure he had completed what he had committed to!

In today's society it's easy to become faceless and almost disappear. The web is infamous for this but while the anonymity it has granted people can be positive, it can also be sinister.

Personal commitment is seen by us to be an absolute key.

Of course, we'd love all businesses to be Wardell clients! Failing that we strongly encourage you to find yourself a mentor or confidant. You need to find someone that will hold you accountable to your goals and hopefully even go beyond to helping you shape your goals.

Volume is Good, but Hair is Bad

Imagine you are climbing a mountain.

You've never been there before.

You're fit and have great gear.

But there is something missing.

Something that will make your journey a success.

In fact, it could save your life!

You hire a guide. The guide helps you avoid pitfalls and points you in the right direction, but you are still making decisions.

You are the one climbing the mountain. The guide simply makes the success of the journey more attainable, more realistic, more achievable.

That's what a properly trained business coach or consultant can do for your business.

You are the one that is an expert in your field.

You may have a great location and a strong work ethic.

Your business is growing, but it could be doing more.

Sounds like climbing a mountain.

Just as an experienced 'mountaineering guide' can help you climb a mountain, an experienced 'business guide' can help you on your journey of making your business a success.

You will still be running your business, but your guide will supply you with tools to help your business grow.

The major thing to remember is quality and quantity always need to seek a balance. You need to have both. Your business survival and life success depend on it. High quality and high quantity. It may sound like a tough recipe, but we believe you can do it!

Chapter 5

Bring it Home

What does 'bring it home' mean?

What we are getting at here is a discussion about the separation of your business and work life with your personal and home life. Believe us, there is plenty of difference of opinion on this issue. Some say to leave the office at the office. Other experts would argue that it is incredibly positive to share what happens at the office with your partner at home.

Our goal here is not to become involved or embroiled in a debate that takes us away from the overall goal of becoming more effective and efficient with our time. That being said, it is very important to see that we can't easily switch ourselves off from one arena to the next.

One of the key differences that we use in the Wardell program for Business Development is that we start by building a personal mission, vision and values with a business owner. For some owners, that seems completely backwards. Why would we start with the personal when it is my business that needs attention?

If you haven't seen the movie Karate Kid, you should rent it. This classic 1980's movie featured a young teenager, Daniel (played by Ralph Macchio), who moves from New Jersey to California. Fitting in is tough and he runs into bullies as he tries to fit in with the new crowd. He turns to karate to defend himself from his new enemies. His exceptionally wise martial arts teacher (Pat Morita) starts by having him paint fences and wax cars however! "Wax on! Wax off!" was the phrase used continually in early stages of training as Daniel wipes his arms in circular motions. Wax cars? What does that have to do with karate? The point was that the learning of that basic skill made the skills that came later much easier to teach. In fact, the movements and motions that were ingrained in these early stages of training became second nature so that Daniel didn't even have to think about these issues…he simply reacted.

Bring it Home

In the same way, the personal foundation sets the stage for a business owner to be mentally prepared to tackle business problems. Working with business owners on their personal missions is exceptionally revealing.

When a business owner writes down what sums him or her up as a person, it changes them. It focuses them. It anchors them. This is what they are and do and believe. Once this personal foundation is in place, the business mission, vision and values flow much more naturally.

As stated, we don't want to enter into a debate about the separation of work and home, but rather to point out what we have seen by experience many times over.

Who you are as a person will affect who you are as a business owner. Who you are as a person will affect who you are as a manager. Who you are as a person will affect you as a stay-at-home dad.

If this is the case, it is extremely important that each of us have a personal mission, vision and values.

Would it be helpful to understand your purpose in life? Would it be useful to be clear on your values? Would it be beneficial to have clearly defined goals that were as inspiring as they were challenging? The answer to each of these questions, of course, is a resounding yes! This kind of knowledge can give you confidence when making important decisions, strength of conviction when times get tough and can act as a guide for building your enterprise the right way, that is, your way.

Your Personal Foundation is a framework, designed to organize and direct your thoughts towards these issues. As important as they are, people rarely give them the time they deserve. The result, compounded over a lifetime, can be an enormous amount of time and energy spent in the wrong direction. The three areas of focus for your Personal Foundation are your purpose (we call that your Mission), your goals (we call them your Vision) and your Values. You need to personally define these key aspects of your life, but don't be too hard on yourself if you don't find your answers right away. It's an evolutionary process that will likely become a lifelong project.

For more information on building a Personal Foundation of your own, just give us a call or drop us a line. There is information at the end of this book on how to get in touch with us. Taking the several minutes to do so is another step forward in changing your world!

Bring it Home

The ex-mayor of New York, Rudolph Giuliani has written a superb book entitled, *Leadership* (2002), the title of which speaks for the content.

One of the things that hits you when reading the book is that Giuliani held himself personally responsible for what happened with his administration. In fact he had a plaque on his desk with the words, 'I'm responsible.' This philosophy was carried right through his entire management group and beyond.

Agree with his politics or not, it's hard not to notice the impact Guilani had on New York, and with events of 9-11, even the world.

It took personal responsibility and old fashioned commitment for Guilani to change the world. It's a lesson worth learning for all of us.

70 Things to do Now That I'm 70

Randy's Story

When my father turned 70 he developed a list entitled, "70+ activities for 70+." The list included all sorts of items, some tame, others a little wild.

One day he went on an excursion with a forestry maintenance worker. They spent the whole day checking out culverts, clearing ditches, along remote stretches of road in the mountains. This came under the category of 'observing men and machines at work - Hydro, logging, sawmill, etc.'

Other items on the list include:

- Writing projects (he's authored two books since turning 65)

- Hiking
- Biking
- Volunteering
- Internet exploration
- Word games

And the list goes on and on.

Why would someone at 70 years old conceive of a list like this?

For my father he thinks 70 is just the beginning. It was his way of establishing his future. It was a powerful indication of his plan for future successes. From a guy who has read 75 books in the last eight months (from paperback to over 1,000 pages), skis over 40 times per year, is still active in the community as a marriage and personal counsellor and plays an active role in his church, there is a lesson to be learned here.

It's certainly never too late to do anything. The world is always there to be discovered. You just need a plan!

So what are the 20 things that you're going to do now that you're 20, 30 things at 30, 40 things at 40, and beyond?

Planning to be Successful

It is laughable when the media portrays someone as an 'overnight' success story. Take a singer for example. Just because they've been signed to a recording label and have now got a song on the top 10 play list does not make them an overnight success.

Their journey usually began at a young age. Singing at family gatherings. Singing at country fairs. Singing in malls before sparse crowds.

In order to accomplish something of value, a long term plan needs to be implemented.

So how do you take inspiration and channel it into something useful?

Be prepared

Do you carry a PDA with you? How about a cell phone, or at the very least, a pen and pad of paper?

Our brains are processing thousands of thoughts every hour.

Many times, our minds are multi-tasking at a level that is hard to keep up with. In order to tap into some of that brainpower, set yourself up to be able to take advantage of these thoughts. Write things down, leave yourself a voicemail, or quickly punch a message into your PDA.

Some people find keeping a daily journal is an excellent avenue for thoughts to be written down. This book has large margins especially for that purpose. Read with a pen handy…write down your ideas immediately. Your best ideas can come at any time!

Once something is written it becomes that much more powerful.

> Patricia worked in a temporary position that she loved. She knew she would have to go back to her 'regular' position when the temporary position ended. She was challenged to write down her goals. She took on this challenge. Her goal was to get a promotion and a better job within six months. She worked hard, took an upgrading course and applied for several jobs. She prepared for the interviews and was offered a new job! She indicated that the writing down of her goal crystallized her vision and provided the dedication and drive in order to meet the goal.

We can't stress enough the power of writing things down, or typing things into a computer, or calling your own voicemail and leaving yourself a message.

Tacit vs. Explicit Knowledge

We promised not a lot of consultant speak, but we do want to sneak in a few theories and terms here that are exceptionally valuable and practical. In addition, you can use them at your next company party or picnic to impress your colleagues!

There are two main categories of knowledge. One is the knowledge that you can find in books or manuals. When you started that first job flipping burgers and read through the manual before your on-the-job training, it was this kind of knowledge. It is called explicit knowledge.

The other form of knowledge is called tacit (or implicit) knowledge. It is the knowledge that is largely stored in people's brains. It's very difficult to get down on paper. The dictionary definition of tacit is, "expressed or carried out without words or speech."

Successful people and organizations are learning how to transfer their tacit knowledge into explicit knowledge.

By writing down your goals, you are taking a big step towards transferring your knowledge into something that is tangible and achievable.

Do you know that others want you to achieve your dreams?

Many sales are missed because sales people don't do something exceptionally simple and basic. That basic step is to ask for the sale. Are you ready to do business with my company? Are you ready to become the proud owner of this car? Ask for the sale.

In the same way we need to ask others to help us be successful. Sound selfish? Don't fall into that trap. People want you to be successful. They feel good when you succeed. If you are successful and someone asks you for help, we bet that you will help them as well. It feels good to give.

Make sure you ask for help. You can ask questions like:

"Would you mind if I called you once a month for your advice on a business issue?"

or

"If I emailed you regarding a management issue I'm having, could you point me in the right direction?"

Ask the questions.

Go for it!

You'll be surprised at the results.

Everything starts at a beginning.

Success doesn't just magically happen.

We challenge you to start your road to success by making a list.

What are you going to do to manage your success?

Others will help you, but you must start the process and work hard.

Good luck!

It's All About Trust

What is trust?

Trust has been defined as assured reliance on the character, ability, strength, or truth of a person or an organization. Stated a different way trust is placing confidence in someone or something.

Why is trust important for your business or organization?

Trust is what can propel your company to be bigger than it is.

Trust in you as the owner and leader can lead to employees taking action that goes well beyond their job description.

The term synergy means that the whole is greater than the sum of the parts. What this means is that if you have five individual people working together instead of just having the output of five individuals it would be like having the output of eight or even more.

How do you get this crazy math working for you?

The fuel for synergy is trust.

If people trust their leaders they themselves will do great things.

If people trust their leaders they also will aspire to win.

If people trust you as their leader they will push your company forward like nothing you have seen before.

Randy's story

In the Management class I teach I spend a week talking about trust and ethics.

One of the most interesting teaching aids that I have found is a video featuring the accounting firm, Arthur Anderson. This accounting firm was at the center of the scandal surrounding Enron in 2001 and was largely blamed for corrupt accounting practises that led to fictitious earning reports and inevitably crippling both companies.

The video did not focus on this much reported story however. Instead this is an older video from the 1980's. The video used the firm Arthur Anderson as an example of ethics in the workplace. It profiled the training that occurred in all levels of the company to bring home the message that ethics was key.

What went so terribly wrong?

How could an organization steeped in ethics and trust lose it all?

Although there are a number of books and hundreds of articles on the subject we may never know the complete answer for sure.

One thing we are willing to speculate on however is this. In the same way that people don't become an overnight success, trust is never built or torn down in short periods of time.

Trust is built one brick at a time.

Trust is built when you do what you say.

You tell employees to be on time, but you are usually running late for meetings.

You suggest that you'll review a job description only to forget about it until the employee asks again.

You expect your employees to be honest, but you take a few items off the shelf without worrying about the accounting hassle of ringing them through the till.

These are all ways of not building trust. They are little things done in the time it would take to make a piece of toast, but they all lead to something much larger.

Consider the story of Sharon.

> Sharon worked in a department of about 10 people. She had seen a number of managers come and go over the past couple of years.
>
> A new young manager came in one day and said he wanted to change things but needed the help of the employees to do so.
>
> Sharon did not believe this. She had heard the story before. Managers wanting input and then just doing what they wanted. She was not going to put too much effort into this new manager's schemes.
>
> As time went on however, Sharon couldn't help but notice something. When this manager said he was going to do something, he did it.

When he asked for input, he actually carefully considered the responses before taking action.

Sharon was asked to take part in an unconventional solution to a business problem in the department. Part of the solution meant that she would have to move her work to a different department for a period of six months.

She thought about it and decided her trust in the manager was strong enough to go for it.

She took on the new role and the business problem was dramatically improved with the new system.

Sharon summed up her experience by saying, this manager built up trust by doing what he said he was going to do. Not just once, but consistently over time.

It is not any more complicated than that.

You must do what you said you were going to do.

If you have that as an internal mantra and then practise it every day your company will move mountains.

In the previous story, Sharon had every opportunity to undermine the new process that the manager was trying to implement. She could have crippled that project. Instead her trust in the manager not only made the department run smoother, it also led to a more fulfilling role for Sharon and a better process for other departments as well.

This is a perfect illustration of synergy.

Regardless of what your math teacher taught you, one plus one does not always have to equal two!

Managing by principle is quite different than managing by rules.

If you want to read an excellent book on principle-based management, Stephen Covey's book, titled *Principle Centered Leadership,* is a must read.

When people operate by rules, they are conducting themselves based on a set of right and wrong that can actually become highly cumbersome. For example, a clerk in the return department of a store arguing the customer has not followed the return policy to the letter and therefore the company cannot accept the return is operating in a rule-based environment.

In the same situation, if there is a general policy, the employee is left to make a determination of what should be done. What is done in one situation may even be different at another time with other circumstances.

In the Wardell system we strongly encourage companies to have systems and procedures for just about everything in their operation.

Does this go against principle-based management? No, not at all. The more you can structure your business, the more successful you can be.

We strongly believe that you can have a highly structured business and still have a company run by principles rather than rules.

Taken too far, rules can limit, not free.

Trust is the tool that allows systems like principle-based management to work.

So how can you get the fuel of trust to propel your business or organization forward?

Take your 'toast time' each day and follow through on a commitment.

Make sure your commitments are recorded so you can follow up.

We believe trust will fuel some of the most successful companies in the future decades.

Check in with us in 2020 and we'll see how we did on this prediction!

HOW TO CHANGE THE WORLD WHILE WAITING FOR YOUR TOAST

Chapter 8

Do the POLC-A

Every book needs a chapter on management theory right? Hey, don't skip forward; this will be good for you!

As discussed in an earlier chapter, the business owner must act as a manager to break through the glass ceiling that separates him or her from true business growth.

They must become less of a mechanic and more of a manager of the mechanic shop. This is not an easy transition for some. In fact it's impossible for some and they shouldn't even try.

But those of you who truly want to grow your business must begin to think like a manager.

In order to properly understand how to run your company, organization, department, or even manage your home life, an understanding of the keys to management is critical.

As we've worked with business owners in different industries and different sizes, the missing pieces of the success puzzle are usually found in one of these areas.

The pillars of management are:

Planning

Organizing

Leading

Controlling

We've added an A. That's for **A**ttitude!

You spell that out and you have the word, POLC-A.

The polka is a dance form that many of you will be familiar with. For those that aren't, it's a form of music and dance that is distinguished by accordion players, lots of food and a lot of clapping!

In any event, if you can remember the polka, you can remember POLC-A!

So, what does each of these terms mean and why are they important? Let's take a more in-depth look.

Planning

Planning is one of the key areas that can set your company apart from your competition. Most companies don't spend a lot of time planning. They deal with issues as they come up.

Most of us have heard the terms reactive and proactive.

In a business setting, being reactive means reacting to issues as they arise. Putting out fires. Always dealing with issues and problems. The more we speak with business owners the more we find that most businesses are caught in the reactive trap.

Being proactive means that you are taking the first step. You are attacking a problem even before it begins. Sounds great in theory right? But honestly, who has the time to attack issues? As a business owner or manager you feel that you're under the gun all day long, every day and some weeks it's seven days per week.

We have helped companies turn this around. We start by showing the company owner how they currently use their time.

Time management is the key to accomplishing any complex task. It puts you in the driver's seat, giving you control over your life. People sometimes react negatively to the notion of time management, arguing that it is impossible or even wasteful to try to organize their time, but we are absolutely convinced they are wrong. Time management is the backbone of self-mastery. It allows you to live your life 'on purpose' by giving you control over your destiny like nothing else can.

Think of a scale. On one side are the hours you 'spend' running your business, and on the other side are the hours you 'invest' improving your business. If you are like most business owners, then right now the scale is probably tipped in favour of your 'spent' time. Your day is likely spent making sales calls, handling customer complaints, and producing products. Our goal is to slowly but surely, tip the scale in favour of your 'invested' time, freeing you to do more valuable work.

To make this happen, you first need to get a hold of your daily schedule. If your daily routine varies, depending on whatever seems to be most important at any given time, then setting aside time to invest in your business will remain a low priority for you. Something else will always take precedent. A customer will need to be called back, your employees will need your help, a package will need to be delivered, and so forth.

Do the POLC-A

The backbone of time management is scheduling. Operating on a schedule forces you to make time for the things you know are important but have trouble getting around to. This does not mean you can never break your schedule. You are in charge, not the schedule. If something new takes priority then by all means, make an adjustment. Just don't make it a habit. When you adjust your schedule you are making a proactive decision. This is still a form of time management and is completely different from operating without a schedule. When you deal with things as they come, you are reacting to, and consequently being controlled by, your environment.

There are plenty of things we have no control over, but one thing we can control is the way we spend our time. It may seem as if you have little control over this as well some days, but in truth, this is the one place you have ultimate control. Certainly you will be influenced to spend your time in certain ways, but the final decision to act is always up to you. Cherish that authority; it is the key to personal and professional success.

A common argument against planning is that if you set out a plan for yourself or your company you are wasting your time because plans rarely turn out the way they were intended.

In actual fact, studies have shown that companies that plan inevitably outperform companies that don't. Why? Even a huge ship turns in the water with a small rudder. It's impossible to steer a ship when it's at rest. But when it's moving, just a slight turn of the rudder will change the ship's direction. Planning is the same. By setting out personal plans and business plans you've set your direction and have a focus. Yes, you may change your plans, but that's ok. It's really the action that the plan has provoked that will propel you and your company.

Organizing

Organizing is so key we have given it an entire chapter of its own (see Chapter 10, 'The freedom of structure'). Suffice it to say here that organization is one of the most overlooked places in small business today. Without organizational structure, however, the business will simply implode. It is an absolute key.

Leading

Leading is a subject that is worth a book on it's own but we'll make do with a few paragraphs here.

Leading is all about example.

The previous chapter on trust really captures a lot of the traits we believe are key if you want to portray solid leadership.

You must be trusted if you expect to lead.

So how do you build that level of confidence?

In very simple terms, it's all about 'walking the talk' and not having a separate set of standards for management and another for staff.

A retail company was working towards improving their image and they decided that the staff needed to be outfitted in uniforms like golf shirts with the company logo etc.

One of the most important discussions that company had as a leadership team was what they should wear to provide leadership on this issue.

It's simple things like this that help employees of an organization feel that there is a sense of team and belonging.

Controlling

There is a misperception that control is all about money. Control can be about money, but it certainly doesn't have to be.

There are three main forms of control. They are feedforward, concurrent, and feedback.

Feedforward control is all about gaining some level of control in a situation before it becomes a problem.

Let's take an example like hiring a new employee.

When is the absolute best time to screen out employees that are going to be an issue for your company? After they've worked with you for three years and caused you a lot of grief? No, of course not. The absolute best time for your business to screen out employees is before you hire them!

Many companies get themselves into a bind by not having standard hiring practises, standard interview questions or any hiring practise whatsoever. We don't care if you have only one employee or one hundred. You need a plan. By simply taking some time to write down questions and think about what kind of responses you are looking for you will be further ahead than most.

Also, make sure you do your reference checks! If a prospective employee won't give you a reference that you can easily contact from a previous job, the red flags should be waving at 100 miles per hour.

Do the POLC-A

This kind of control is called feedforward because you are controlling a situation before it becomes a problem.

Concurrent control is managing situations as they happen. So in very simple terms, if you see an employee doing something incorrectly, by taking a minute to explain the problem and rectify it in real time, you are practising concurrent control.

A very simple technique for concurrent control as it relates to working with staff is called the 'coaching sandwich.' It's effective whether you're working with six-year-old soccer players on your team or a group of PhD's on a research project.

The coaching sandwich works like this. First you provide a compliment on what the employee is doing correctly. (That's the first layer of bread.) Then you apply some direction and make a direct statement on what the employee was doing incorrectly and how it could be corrected. (That's the meat!) Then you compliment the employee again. (That's the other piece of bread).

And voila! You have a coaching sandwich. Here's how it works in real life. Business owner Val notices employee Jan not greeting customers as they go through her till. She pulls Jan aside and lets her know that she really appreciates her positive attitude since coming to work for the company. (Slice one!). Then Val explains that each customer must be greeted in a certain way. For example Val might say, "I noticed that although you smiled at the customer, you did not greet them. What we need to do as a company is greet each customer and ensure they have found everything they need." She would then complete the coaching sandwich by saying that she is proud of the effort Jan is making to be an excellent team player.

It's simple to use and highly effective. We spend very little time telling people what they've done right! The coaching sandwich forces you to point out the positive as well as the negative.

This is a solid example of concurrent control.

Finally, feedback control is the most common form of control used largely because it's the easiest. Keeping with the employee theme, feedback control would be the yearly job evaluation. If your company isn't completing job evaluations on a regular basis, it's a good thing to do. At the very least, it provides some feedback to the employee. The drawback however, is the length of time between this feedback. If you focus on practicing feedforward control and concurrent control you'll be much further ahead.

Attitude

To conclude our POLC-A dance we have the word attitude.

I love the phrase, "Your attitude determines your altitude."

Think about it. Above all else, how you perceive things, your desire, your vision, your drive…your attitude determines your altitude.

How high do you want to fly?

How far do you want to take your business?

It's your attitude that will make all the difference.

HOW TO CHANGE THE WORLD WHILE WAITING FOR YOUR TOAST

Chapter 9

10 Minutes to Learn the Tkatchev

Mark's story

There was one pivotal event that changed my approach to coaching like no other. Not only did it change my approach to coaching, but it formed the approach that we now use with business owners in the Wardell program.

In my previous life, I was a competitive gymnastics coach. I loved the sport…still do. For me it represents the best in human physical potential. Gymnastics paid for my university degree and became my profession of choice upon graduating. As time went on, however, I began to see more clearly what it was that I truly loved about coaching. As fascinated as I was with the sport of gymnastics, it was the challenge of fulfilling human potential that got me out of bed every morning.

The real shift in my thinking came one afternoon at a gymnastics conference. I was watching a Russian video of a young girl learning a high-level move, called a Tkatchev, on the uneven bars. The girl had never tried the move before, yet within 10 minutes she was completing the move on her own. Amazed, the person filming the event asked the coach how it was possible for the young gymnast to have learned the move in such a short period of time. The coach's response will stay with me forever. With a puzzled look he replied, "10 minutes to learn the Tkatchev, but 10 years to prepare to learn the Tkatchev."

At that instant I suddenly realized what my fellow coaches and I had been doing wrong. We were spending far too much time working on skills, and not nearly enough time preparing for them. The following year I took my athletes right out of competition and returned to the basics. For a full year we did nothing but physically prepare our bodies and our minds. In fact, we did very little actual gymnastics. It was a radical move and I received my share of flack from the coaching community for it, but I would soon forget all of that. The following year, I began to introduce gymnastics skills back into the curriculum and an amazing thing happened. Every one of my athletes learned at a faster rate than I had ever thought possible. Not only did the skills come faster, they were of superior quality. As an added bonus, our injury rate decreased by over 90 percent.

I wasn't the only one to see that Russian video, yet when we returned to competition, we were unstoppable. If I brought three athletes to a meet, they came 1st through 3rd. If I brought six athletes, they came 1st through 6th. It was amazing, but it taught me a valuable lesson as well…one that continues to guide me to this day.

"The strength of your foundation determines the height of your potential." In other words, the level of success you will be able to obtain in life is predetermined by the quality and quantity of your preparation.

It's a simple philosophy that I always thought I lived by, but until the day of that video, I know that I did not.

The traditional learning method that I had been using was essentially flawed. In essence it was a roadblock to learning that I had to either get around, over or through.

What are your roadblocks to learning? What's keeping you from being more successful? What's keeping your company from growing?

A lot of times the viewer in us comes up with many reasons why we can't be successful.

After all, it's not just the world around us that is trying to hold us back, we do it to ourselves as well. Visible or invisible, you ask anyone and they can tell you at least one thing that they have trouble with. As small as allergies or as big as cancer. From a fear of public speaking to unpreventable tics. These are not meant to be callous statements, but simply a statement of fact.

Success can be had at any level of human experience.

We live in a time when it's easy to shirk responsibility. It's not our problem. We've heard the excuses. "I had a rough childhood." "I have a learning disability."

Here's the straightforward reality. If you concentrate on your problem you will never find a solution.

You must get on with achieving your goal. The list of successful people that have visible disabilities and still succeeded is truly amazing.

10 Minutes to Learn the Tkatchev

Rick Hanson propelled himself around the world on his wheelchair to raise money for spinal cord research. Today he is a business leader and shares his inspirational story of overcoming odds with thousands of people each year.

Michael J. Fox suffers from Parkinson's disease. This award winning actor continues to fight through his illness and provide people with the gift of laughter through his work.

Robert Schuller is a motivational speaker and founder of the Crystal Cathedral in California. He made a statement that is as true today as when he first starting using it in the 1980's. "Turn your scars into stars," was the anthem.

What are you doing to turn your scars into stars?

How can you take a problem and turn it into a solution?

How can you learn to learn?

Remember…we want you to work hard. That is an overlooked trait in today's society. We must work hard. But equally important is to work at doing the right things.

That's what learning to learn is all about.

Prepare yourself for greatness by getting the basic fundamentals of your business sorted out.

Is your business plan in place?

What are your personal goals?

We'll look forward to reading your story of success against the odds in a future business publication!

Chapter 10

The Freedom of Structure

The word 'structure' can sound foreboding. It can sound ominous. It actually should be just the opposite.

Structure can buy you freedom. Structure should be your friend! Structure is at the heart of the Wardell system and is how we have turned many businesses around.

The dictionary describes structure as: "The way in which parts are arranged or put together to form a whole."

This definition gives a glimpse into the way we want you to view structure. It's the solid foundation onto which everything else is built. When your house or apartment was built, the workers first began with the hole in the ground. This hole, however, was exceptionally critical in the overall success or failure of your home. The materials used in the construction of the foundation are what everything else rests on.

It's the same in your business and the same in your life. What is the foundation of your business? What are the principles that you've built your company on? When we visit with companies, we are no longer surprised to find that many firms simply don't have any. There are always been urgent things to do…customers to take care off…employee problems to deal with. There was no time to deal with things like the foundation of the business.

Thinking like that is very typical. Thinking like that is also why 80 percent plus of business ventures eventually fail!

Get organized!

Truly great accomplishments come about through the intelligently coordinated efforts of truly great people. If we work hard and if we invest our time wisely we can do a lot on our own, but when motivated people come together to pursue a common goal, the results go far beyond the sum of their individual efforts. Two people working together in an organized fashion will always out-produce two people working separately. So how do we get people working together in an organized fashion? Through management.

The purpose of management is to connect people with order, which, for your average business owner, makes it an oxymoron. Many business owners say that the most frustrating part of running their business is dealing with their staff. Why? Because people are not predictable.

People have their own agendas which may or may not have anything to do with the success of your business. People bring creativity, knowledge, skills, and productivity to a business, but rarely do they bring order. That is, unless you plan it that way.

Order is the product of good management. It lets people work cooperatively and efficiently towards a common goal. It's an inspiring goal. In fact, it's a necessary goal. But it will only become a realistic goal if your business is highly organized.

OK, so you want to put some structure into your business…but how?

When you bought your car, it came with an owner's manual that showed you how it works and how to take care of it. Unfortunately, your business didn't come with such a manual. You had to figure it out on your own. But what if you did have such a manual? Think about it.

If you wanted to sell your business, what would a tried and true manual that explained exactly how and why your business works be worth to a prospective buyer? Quite a bit.

If you wanted to expand your business, wouldn't it be helpful if your employees had a reference that contained the answers to their business questions? Absolutely.

And what about you? How valuable would such a reference book be to you? Would you benefit from a book that ensured the reliable operation of your business, even when you were not there? Of course.

We are often asked, "What is the single most important piece of advice you'd give to a prospective business owner?" And our answer is always the same.

Get everything you possibly can out of your head and onto paper.

Knowledge is power, but inside your head, it can only serve you. On paper (better yet, on a computer), its value knows no limits. It can be used to train one person or one thousand. It's up to you.

The Freedom of Structure

What do you want to do with your company?

Grow it?

Sell it?

Franchise it?

Take it public?

Acquire other companies?

Set it up to run on its own?

Wherever you want to take your company, if you really want to succeed, you need to begin by getting it organized. Get clear on your direction and carefully document your plans for getting there. If you don't, you're setting yourself up for failure. But if you take the time to set it up properly, the sky's the limit.

HOW TO CHANGE THE WORLD WHILE WAITING FOR YOUR TOAST

Decision Making – Toast Style!

"Whenever you see a successful business, someone once made a courageous decision."

Peter F. Drucker,
Management author

All action begins with a decision. It's a simple concept, but it's surprising how many people get stopped before they begin because they just can't make a decision. Luckily, decision-making is a learned skill. This is good news because it means no matter how good or bad you are at it right now, you can always get better.

The first thing to remember when faced with a decision is that while some are important, most are trivial. Most people spend far too much time making trivial decisions and not nearly enough time making important ones. Begin thinking of those smaller decisions as a pizza pocket that only needs 10 seconds in the microwave. The bigger 'bagel' sized decisions take a little longer, but still have a limited time frame. Don't get caught doing nothing! Even a wrong decision can propel you forward in the big picture.

This is a story of two best friends, Blake and Tanner. These two boys were so much alike. Everyone that met them assumed they were brothers.

Blake's parents decided early on that part of raising a young boy into becoming a self-assured man, was giving him an early start on decision-making skills. They always gave Blake decisions. Anything from what to wear to school, to what sport he would like to play, to what restaurant to eat at.

Tanner's parents decided that all decisions were easier made by an adult, keeping in mind what is best for Tanner. At the end of high school, Tanner couldn't make any decisions for himself. He was always afraid to make a mistake, and as such, continued through his life figuring out ways to not make a decision, and avoid making a mistake. He now works for a dictatorship style company going nowhere quickly.

Decision Making – Toast Style!

Blake, on the other hand, is the CEO of a multi-million dollar corporation, handling his daily dose of decisions with ease. He now says, "Everyone makes bad decisions in life, but you cannot run a business if you are always sitting on the fence. Things need to be decided on quickly and then you can move forward and tackle the next decision. My dad has always told me that any decision is better than indecision, and I believe it to be true."

The amount of time and energy you devote to making a decision should be in direct relation to the importance of that decision. If the outcome will have no meaningful impact on your life or your business, then either make the decision instantly, or don't make it at all. For example, if you spend more than a few seconds deciding what brand of chewing gum to buy, you are wasting your time. It may seem like a small thing, after all, what are a few minutes here and there, but it is surprising how those minutes add up. For example, if you can eliminate just 15 minutes a day worth of trivial decision making, you will gain back the equivalent of over two weeks worth of eight-hour workdays per year.

On the other hand, it is important to take enough time when making important decisions. For example, purchasing a home is one of the most important financial decisions many people make, and yet they'll make it in a matter of hours, or even minutes, without conducting any significant research.

To better manage this aspect of decision-making, learn to set time limits. If the decision is relatively unimportant, give yourself a maximum amount of time to make it. For example, you might give yourself a maximum of 20 seconds to choose the brand of chewing gum you will purchase. For more significant decisions, you could also set a minimum amount of time for research and contemplation as well. For example, you might take an extra few days to have a home properly inspected and appraised before deciding whether or not to buy it.

Once you have made your decision, stick to it. Most people let the process go on and on by waffling back and forth on a decision. They make a decision, but almost any information to the contrary could sway them in a new direction.

It is also important to realize that you don't have to make all of the decisions that come your way. When it comes to your business, you should only need to make the important decisions. If someone else can make the decision, let him. It is important that your employees take on the responsibility of making their own decisions whenever possible. So if an employee comes to you with a dilemma, offer your advice, but

Decision Making – Toast Style!

try to leave the decision with them. If you do this often enough, people will eventually learn to make their own decisions without involving you.

When a decision is too important to leave to anyone else, make sure you gather all of the necessary information prior to making it. In general, the more important the decision, the more information you should gather. But how do you determine the level of importance to place on a decision?

To determine how important a decision is, try the following.

1. Ask yourself what the downside would be to making the wrong decision. How damaging could the worst-case scenario be?

2. Ask yourself if you could live with this or if it would destroy you?

3. Identify the upside. What would the best-case scenario be like?

4. Now, answer the following question. If you could flip a coin and one of these two scenarios would instantly come into existence, would you do it? Would the benefits of the upside be worth the risk of the downside? The easier it would be to base the decision on a coin toss, the less important the decision is and the less

time and energy you should put into making it. Of course the opposite is also true. The more difficult it would be to make the decision on a coin toss, the more important the decision is and the more time and energy you should put into making it.

Over the next two weeks, practice giving yourself time limits for making decisions. And no matter what, stick to them.

Using Your Intuition

Sometimes you won't have access to all of the information you'd like, or you'll be too pressed for time to gather it. Situations like this force you to rely primarily on your intuition. Luckily, if it is approached correctly this can be an effective tool for decision making. Certainly if you have the time it is usually a good idea to do your due diligence, but your intuition may be more valuable than you realize.

The trick to getting your intuition working for you is to ask yourself the right questions. The right questions will help you see your problems as opportunities for improvement, putting you in the right frame of mind for identifying meaningful solutions. For example, if you know you will be late with an

Decision Making – Toast Style!

order for an important client and you are not sure how to handle the situation, imagine the ideal outcome and then search for a way of getting there. You might ask yourself, "How could we be late with the order and have our client appreciate it?" It may seem outrageous, but this approach allows you to become solution oriented rather than problem oriented. One possible solution might be to include some extra features with the order. The implication would be that you kept the order a little longer to upgrade a VIP customer. Another might be to hand deliver the order, ensuring it arrives in perfect condition. Again, this could be a special service you provide only to VIP customers.

The nature of a question is that it demands an answer. Without an answer, you are left hanging. Consequently, your subconscious will work overtime to provide you with that answer. Your first thoughts may or may not produce your final solution, but if you remain confident you will eventually find it. Write down the various random solutions you come up with, even if they seem outrageous. You may be surprised at where they lead you.

HOW TO CHANGE THE WORLD WHILE WAITING FOR YOUR TOAST

Breaking Down the Barriers

Great achievers are endowed with a tremendous drive. They go after their dreams with an uncommon intensity and they refuse to give up until they have exhausted each and every possibility. To do so would be unthinkable to them. They persevere until they succeed and then people watch them with envy and say, "Boy, are those people ever lucky!" What stops all of us from doing the very same thing? Even though most of us are aware of the value of perseverance, it seems that once we encounter an obstacle or a barrier presenting a significant challenge, we often give up. In this section we're going to examine the major 'barriers to success.' We'll see how they stop us from reaching our potential and we'll learn how to break through them to achieve the success we deserve.

Consider these facts:

- Virginia Wade played in Wimbledon for 15 years straight and lost the prestigious title all 15 years. She came back in 1977 to win!
- Henry Ford made and lost his money five times before he finally succeeded.
- Beethoven was deaf and still composed beautiful masterpieces.
- Albert Einstein was told at a young age that he was a slow learner, and some teachers even considered him retarded.
- Abraham Lincoln was raised in poverty.
- Colonel Sanders was broke at 65. He used his social security check to start Kentucky Fried Chicken (KFC).

Barrier 1 - Excuses

Success is hard work and the greater the goal, the greater the challenge. Knowing this can make the idea of failure an extremely painful thought. After all, who wants to put everything they have into something that doesn't work out? It's demoralizing and it's humiliating. So what do people do? They make excuses. If you can find a really good reason

Breaking Down the Barriers

why failure is not your fault, you can deflect the blame away from yourself.

"Mary didn't get back to me in time to finish the report."

"The competition is bigger so they have more resources."

"The competition is smaller so they're more flexible."

The rewards of success are everything you imagine them to be and more, but the journey is long and hard and the possibility of failure will always exist. Often, excuses can seem like a less painful alternative. They let you avoid the long hard journey to success and they soften the blow of failure. But do they really?

In the short term, excuses can appear to offer a solution, but in reality they're just a smoke screen, causing you to walk right into failure without even noticing. Excuses are unconscious yet clever little acts of self-sabotage that will keep you from achieving your goals, if you let them. We've all been there, we've all made excuses instead of following through with our commitments, and in the end we were no closer to our goals than when we started.

But we've all experienced success as well. We all know the feeling of a plan coming together. The feeling that nothing in the world can stop us. The feeling of success. Hold on to that feeling. Its memory can help to pull you through the next time the stakes are high, your reputation is on the line and you're tempted to start looking for excuses.

Let's have a look at how we use excuses to pull ourselves off track and at some of the solutions we can use to fight back.

The Unfair Advantage Excuse

If we look hard enough, we can always find someone faster, smarter, better connected, and so on, than ourselves. The "Unfair Advantage Excuse" justifies giving up on our goals by pointing out any and all advantages others have over us. It's tempting to use the Unfair Advantage Excuse when faced with competition that seems to start from a superior position. After all, how can we be expected to succeed in the face of such odds?

One example of the Unfair Advantage Excuse says that successful people operate on an inside track. It's a kind of conspiracy theory implying that successful people have an unfair advantage over everyone else, because they have access to special information. "It's not how hard you work, it's who

Breaking Down the Barriers

you know." Does who you know help? Sure, but it's no reason to give up.

It's convenient to think that there's a magic formula for success. It takes all of the pressure off of us by falsely implying that success is quick and easy. It's a great excuse for giving up or not trying, but of course, it's not true.

No, the problem is not the availability of information. There are thousands upon thousands of excellent books on the market that can provide you with the latest and greatest techniques for team building, time management, people management, financial planning, networking, and anything else you might want to know about. More books, in fact, than you could possibly read in a lifetime. On top of this, the lives of the world's most successful men and women have been documented in biographies for all to learn from. In fact, practically every piece of information that you could ever want to know has been written down in a book. If that's not enough, there are audio and videotapes, CD ROM's, the Internet, your own personal network of friends and colleagues, and even the media, which can provide you with still more information.

No, we cannot blame our disappointments on a lack of access to information. Everything that we need to know in order to succeed beyond our wildest dreams is readily available to us. We may have to do a little digging, but it literally is just sitting there, right in front of us. We can have it any time we want if we are willing to do the work to get it. The problem is that most of us never take that next step. Our dreams can become our reality if we'll only step forward and grab hold of them, but instead, we wait for them to come to us. The crazy thing is that deep down we all know what we need to do in order to achieve success, yet only a few of us ever fully take on the challenge.

The same holds true when we allow ourselves to focus on our limitations. It's tempting to blame our upbringing, our status, our intelligence, our education, our environment, or even our luck when things don't go as planned. We blame the economy, we blame our customers, or we blame our staff.

> Helen Keller was deaf, blind, and without speech since an illness struck her at 19 months. If Helen was able to achieve such greatness, how can we use our excuses as legitimate reasons for failure?

The truth is that there are countless examples to refute each of these excuses and more. No matter what your situation, someone else has gone from where you are now to the life of his or her dreams.

Breaking Down the Barriers

That's exciting, because it means that if you're willing to make the same commitment, then you can do it too. It's really just a question of what price you're willing to pay. How badly you want to succeed at something will determine how much effort you are willing to put into it.

Can the hand dealt to you by life make it harder for you to succeed? Of course it can. For some, the road is longer and harder than it is for others. It's a shame and it's not fair, but it's the way it is. It's all right to feel sorry for yourself on occasion, but if you continuously focus on your shortcomings you'll never discover your true potential. It might temporarily make you feel better, but if it causes you to give up on your dreams, it's just not worth it.

So how do we avoid the temptation to make excuses? By taking accountability for our own actions. When we stop making excuses for ourselves, a world of possibilities opens up to us. Why? Because if we have no one but ourselves to blame for our failures then we have no one but ourselves to credit for our successes. If the only limitations we have are self-imposed, then the power to remove them rests with us as well.

Just remember these two simple rules.

    1. You're completely in charge of your own life.

2. You're the best person for the job.

Barrier 2 - Procrastination

Procrastination is what we do instead of what we should be doing. It's another form of self-sabotage that causes us to mix up our priorities. The result is that we end up doing all sorts of things, sometimes anything, rather than what really needs to be done. Procrastination kicks in when we have an unpleasant job ahead of us. Perhaps we need to make some cold sales calls or perhaps we need to do our taxes. Suddenly, little unimportant tasks seem very important. Of course we plan to get to that unpleasant job just as soon as we finish everything else, but by the time we get around to it, we're usually rushed for time and end up with a substandard result. Even in the best case scenario, procrastination is a waste of time and energy. The longer you put something off that you know needs to be done, the longer you extend the stress associated with it.

To avoid procrastination, redirect your focus away from the unpleasant task at hand and towards the results of that task. While the task itself might be unpleasant, if it's truly important, the results will be highly rewarding. It is difficult to continuously push yourself to do things that you don't want to do but if you focus on the highly desirable results of your work, you will find yourself drawn into it with much less resistance. It's a shift from short-term thinking to long-term thinking. By looking ahead to the results of your work, you'll find that important tasks becomes less daunting and more urgent...a clear sign that you are beginning to take better control of your own time.

Barrier 3 - Resistance to Change

Why is it so difficult for people to make even the smallest of changes to their lives? If we have the power to make changes for the better, then why don't we? Why do we often carry on in one direction, in the face of evidence that suggests we go in another? What gets in the way?

Pride

It is painful to admit that we are at the root of our own problems. It is much more pleasant to blame our environment or our circumstance than it is to blame ourselves. This is where our pride can get in the way. If we're not careful, pride can make us resistant to change by keeping us from admitting our mistakes to ourselves and to others. This isn't to say that pride is always a bad thing. It's important to be proud of our accomplishments or of the people we care about. We just need to keep it in check.

Your Comfort Zone

In most cases, changing the way we do things means stepping outside of our comfort zone. For many people, that in itself is an unsettling prospect. In order to truly succeed, however, there's just no getting around it. The world will keep changing whether you do or not so if you never venture outside of your comfort zone, you'll eventually be left behind.

The good news is that stepping outside of our comfort zone is, quite literally, child's play. When we were children, the whole world was outside of our comfort zone. We learned and we grew through trial and error. Change was a way of life. As we got older, however, we learned to fit in and to stop experimenting. There's a great deal of pressure in society to blend in…to go with the flow…to not stand out. Successful people have learned to resist that pressure.

Fear

If you are human, then every once in a while you are affected by fear. Fear of the unknown, fear of failure…perhaps even fear of success. Uncontrolled, fear can become a powerful emotion that will stop you dead in your tracks every time you try to get ahead. Once you learn to control it however, fear can become your ally, raising a red flag when you're operating a little too close to the edge.

Fear comes from many places, disguised in many forms and as every coach knows, there's only one way to beat it. You've got to look it squarely in the eyes and see it for what it really is. An illusion. Then you attack. Fear will always back down if you face it head on because the only real power it has is the power you give it. Fear is an internal force, not an external one. While it is often hard to see this, you really do create your own fear. You can create fear and you can eliminate fear. The choice is entirely up to you.

Are we saying that you should blindly charge forward no matter what the consequences? Of course not. You must always use sound judgment when making a decision. On the other hand, if you don't learn to control your fears, they will control you. You, not your fears, are responsible for making decisions in your life.

Smashing Through the Barriers

Following is a simple three-step process that will help you stop making excuses, blast though procrastination, combat fear, and take positive action for yourself and for your business.

Awareness

The reason these artificial barriers have such a powerful effect on our actions is that we don't think of them as artificial. They often seem so real to us that we interpret them as facts, rather than as the illusions they really are. Self-awareness, then, is the first step towards self-improvement. Catching yourself making an excuse, for example, may be all you need to put yourself back on track.

Take Action

The next time you notice yourself searching for a reason to give up on something important, stop what you are doing, reaffirm your commitment to your goals, and do something, no matter how small, to get yourself back on track. This type of positive action refocuses your attention on your goals, and takes your mind off your problems. You can only focus your attention on one thought at a time, so the simple act doing something constructive will help to push you through the negative illusion you have created.

Practice

What you're fighting here is a long-standing, learned behaviour. Essentially, it's a habit. Breaking it will be difficult at first, but it will get easier over time. Sports science has taught us that 21 consecutive repetitions of the same action will create a habit. So keep working at it and before you know it you will have formed the new and significantly more empowering habit of perseverance.

Chapter 13

Taking Action

If you've taken an active role in applying this book, you've already taken action on some key issues.

Your journey to becoming a better manager or business owner has begun. And that is a very important key. It's hard to simply begin, but now that you are there, don't let that momentum slip away. It's a precious thing!

One of the most practical and effective ways for you to maintain that momentum is to work with someone who is willing to be your mentor, coach and business consultant. If you can find this person, you will be much further ahead than trying to do this journey on your own.

It is human nature to put things aside when you get busy. When the struggle of business survival is being fought, long-term planning is not usually top of mind or on your 'to do' list. The reality is that this is precisely the time when you need help the most.

At Wardell we offer a business development system, which includes the services of a highly skilled and experienced personal business consultant. We call it the "Building a Better Business" program.

This program can help guide you safely through the rough times and make the most of the good times by building a solid foundation for your business.

If you don't have anyone that can work with you to accomplish these goals, we'd love to hear from you to see if there is a fit between your company and ours.

You can contact us to tell us your business story, to arrange a speaking engagement, or to discuss how we can work together to build your organization. You can also review the stories and quotes from other business owners on the Wardell website. These will provide you with a better understanding of the journey other business owners are on as they work to fulfill their entrepreneurial dreams!

web:	www.wardell.biz
e-mail:	randy@wardell.biz
	mark@wardell.biz
phone toll free:	1.888.4.WARDELL (92-7335)

Taking Action

The goal of this book has been to illustrate that even small amounts of time, (like the time it would take to make your toast), can be utilized to make your life and business more successful.

As one of our clients stated, "Funny how the little things make such a big difference!"

We've aimed to provide some practical tips and insights into how to grow a successful business and organization.

We trust we've been able to help you visualize and begin to set and meet those goals for your own situation.

We wish you all the greatest success in your business life, home life and all of your relationships and networks.

What direction is your business headed?

We're thinking up, up and up! And remember, the time needed to change your direction is as small as waiting for your toast.

Author profiles

Randy Friesen

Randy Friesen's background includes over 15 years of management experience as a practicing manager and business consultant. In addition, Mr. Friesen is a Management instructor for the School of Business at the British Columbia Institute of Technology, Canada's premier polytechnic institution located in Vancouver, British Columbia.

With experience in unionized and non-unionized management roles as well as a strong relationship with the entrepreneurial community, Mr. Friesen brings a powerful depth and breadth of knowledge to Wardell clients by being able to provide practical 'real life' solutions to problems that business owners face.

He holds a diploma of Marketing Management (Small Business Development Option) and a Bachelor of Technology Degree in Management. He has also completed Post Graduate studies in the area of Knowledge Management from the University of South Australia.

Together with his family, he makes his home in the horse and wine country of the Fraser Valley, just outside of Vancouver, BC.

Mark Wardell

Having reached the national level as a gymnastics coach, Mark Wardell knows what it takes to win. He took that same drive and desire that made him a success in the world of sports and applied it to business. That transition was founded in tremendous sacrifice and vision which became the building blocks for the Wardell Professional Development program.

Years of research, practical application and mentorship training added to Mr. Wardell's formal university education to provide a perspective that is based on solid business principles. This perspective has proven exceptionally applicable in a practical sense for companies as diverse as animation studios and steel fabricators.

Mr. Wardell is propelled by a desire to see businesses succeed. That success lies in the mindset of the business owner. Working one-on-one with business owners, he has revolutionized businesses that have partnered with Wardell Professional Development.

A committed lifelong learner, Mr. Wardell is constantly researching, networking and exploring new ideas with successful people with the goal of continuing to provide Wardell clients with the premier experience and results in business consulting and coaching services.

Company Profile

Our Mission
Wardell Professional Development is a progressive organization, dedicated to helping people achieve their entrepreneurial dreams.

Our Vision
We will continuously seek to become our clients' most valuable and trusted business development resource.

Our Values
We are committed to the pursuit of excellence and the elimination of mediocrity.

We treat others with respect and expect to be treated the same way.

We are dedicated to the philosophy of continuous improvement.

We hold personal and professional integrity as our highest ideal.

We conduct all our affairs with a high degree of professionalism.

We view each problem as a challenge with an opportunity for growth.

We are dedicated to the proliferation of entrepreneurialism, in all its forms.

Taking Action

ISBN 1412035384

42495>